You've probably seen a model of the solar system that looks something like this.

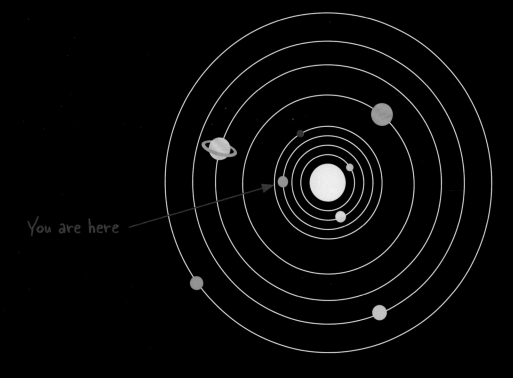

You are here

It's a pretty good model.
It's simple, it's colorful,
It's easy to understand.

It only has one problem:
IT IS A LIE.

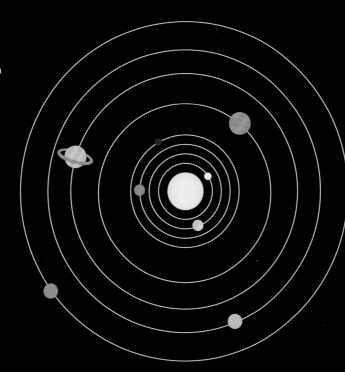

The planets DO NOT
all hang out together.

They DO NOT almost
bump into each other
when they pass by.

VERY, VERY, VERY, VERY

FAR AWAY

A Journey Through the Amazing Scale of the Solar System

MIKE VAGO

THE EXPERIMENT
NEW YORK

Lying is never okay.
Except sometimes it is.

Just about every model or map has to lie about one thing: size. As you may have noticed, this model is **MUCH SMALLER** than the real solar system. But that's a good thing—you can't have a book the size of the solar system. How would it fit in your room?

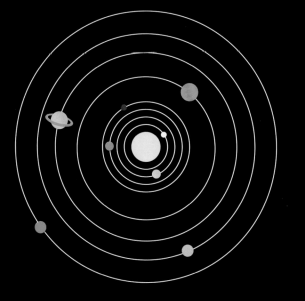

That's where SCALE comes in!

When we **HAVE** to lie about size, scale keeps us honest. "Scale" means everything gets bigger or smaller by the **SAME AMOUNT**. If you drew yourself at half scale, your head would be half as big, your nose would be half as big, your left foot would be half as big. . . . You get the idea.

The simplest scale is **1 to 1.** That means everything is exactly life-size. The average person's pupils are 63 millimeters apart, so these are also 63 millimeters apart:

 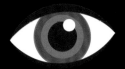

A **10-to-1** scale shows everything at **one tenth** its normal size. Here are those same eyes, at 10 to 1:

SIDE NOTE: We'll use the metric system in this book, because metric is all about multiples of 10 and we're going to do A LOT of multiplying by 10!

Let's scale down some BIGGER things.

Your desk is **NOT** bigger than an elephant. We just made it look that way by using different scales. But at least we were **HONEST** about that!

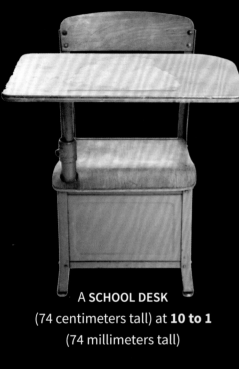

A **SCHOOL DESK**
(74 centimeters tall) at **10 to 1**
(74 millimeters tall)

A taller-than-average
AFRICAN ELEPHANT (4 meters tall)
at **100 to 1** (4 centimeters tall)

The **EIFFEL TOWER**
(324 meters tall)
at **10,000 to 1** (32.4 millimeters tall)

Now let's scale down something REALLY massive. Something like . . .

... the SUN.

This is not the real Sun.
This is the Sun at 10,000,000,000-to-1 scale.

The real Sun is TEN BILLION times bigger
than this picture.

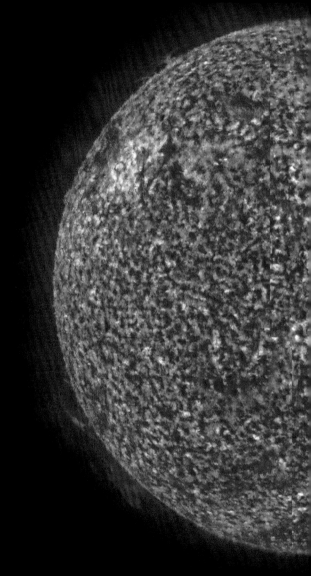

It's hot. Like a giant nuclear fusion reactor, the Sun turns 622 million metric tons of hydrogen into helium **EVERY SECOND.** When the hydrogen runs out (in about 5 billion years), the Sun will turn from a yellow dwarf star into a red giant.

It's weird. The band They Might Be Giants once sang, "The Sun is a mass of incandescent gas." This is false. (The band issued a retraction.) The Sun is made of **PLASMA**—a state of matter so hot that electrons fly away from their atoms and go off on their own for a while.

And it's really, REALLY big. The Sun weighs 333,000 times as much as Earth. All that mass gives the Sun a **LOT** of gravitational pull, which keeps the planets in orbit around it . . . even though they're **VERY, VERY, VERY FAR AWAY.**

How far away? Here we go . . .

Here's the Sun at a 100,000,000,000-to-1 scale.

That's 10 times smaller than our last scale!

The real Sun is **one hundred billion** times the size of this yellow dot.

One centimeter on this page is a **MILLION** kilometers in real life!

Now let's go find the rest of the planets.

Unfold the left and right sides, and
buckle up—we're going to Mercury.

And here's Earth.

Earth is really far away from the Sun, 149.6 million km, to be precise.
Earth is also 10 times its true scale!

This tiny dot is the Moon.

Six pages and 150 million km from the Sun, and we've only seen three planets, one moon, and a lot
of empty space. Even at a hundred billion to one, the planets are too far apart to fit on one foldout.

When you're done, fold these pages back up.
It's time for a a closer look at . . .

. . . THE INNER PLANETS at
100,000,000-to-1 scale

The first four planets have a lot in common: They're all made of rock, they're all closer to the Sun (and to each other) than the gas giants are, and they all look like tiny little dust specks in the two models you've seen so far!

But we can change the scale and take a closer look. Up close, these four are as different from each other as they are far away from each other. These are all real photos of the planets, taken by NASA.

Mercury is hot. And cold. And medium?

Days to orbit the Sun: 87.969 Earth days

Length of day: 58.646 Earth days

Favorite Beatle: George

Gravity: 38% Earth gravity

Atmosphere: None

Moons: None

Temperature range: −180°C to 430°C

How we might live there one day: Most of Mercury is incredibly hot, and the poles are incredibly cold, but there are spots in between that are incredibly medium. Mercury doesn't have an atmosphere exactly, just a thin exosphere that's mostly made of sodium, hydrogen, and oxygen—but nowhere near enough to support human life. On the plus side, the closest planet to the Sun would be a terrific place to build solar panels.

Venus is hot. And cloudy. And hot.

Days to orbit the Sun: 224.7 Earth days

Length of day: 243.025 Earth days

Gravity: 90.4% Earth gravity

Claim to fame: The brightest planet in our night sky. Also great at tic-tac-toe.

Atmosphere: 95.6% CO_2, 3.5% nitrogen

Moons: None

Average temperature: 462°C

How we might live there one day: Venus' surface is so hot that most metals melt there. Not a great place to build a house! But just like on Earth, the atmosphere gets cooler the higher you go. One day, we might build giant hot-air balloons that float high above the surface. Or super-tall structures like Cloud City in *The Empire Strikes Back*.

Here is Venus.

108.2 million km from the Sun, and shown at
10 times the correct scale so you can see it!

Any planets on this page? Nope.

We hope it's starting to sink in: The planets are very, very, very far away.

In between them is nothing but empty space. So much space, it takes up most of this book!

Here's Earth! Can you spot your house?

Days to orbit the Sun: 365.256 (That .256 is why we have leap year.)

Length of day: 24 hours

Gravity: 100% Earth gravity

Atmosphere: 78.08% nitrogen, 20.95% oxygen, 0.93% argon, 0.04% CO_2 (and rising)

Moons: The Moon. (They must have run out of names.)

Temperature range: −89.2°C to 56.7°C

We already live here. Earth is the only planet known to host life. But we may yet discover life on other planets, and if we spread to other planets ourselves, we could bring all kinds of Earth life with us. In the meantime, we have to take care of our environment. Living on other planets will be a **LOT** harder to do!

Look up! It's the Moon! Between 1969 and 1972, NASA sent six missions to the Moon. Each time, two astronauts walked on the surface. Only those twelve people have ever visited a celestial body besides Earth. So far.

Mars' moons look like giant potatoes.

We just thought you should know.

Days to orbit the Sun: 686.97 Earth days

Length of day: 24 hours, 37 minutes, 22 seconds

State bird: Scarlet tanager

Gravity: 37.6% Earth gravity

Atmosphere: 95% CO_2, 2.6% nitrogen, 1.9% argon

Moons: Phobos and Deimos. Possibly asteroids that got sucked into Mars' gravity. Probably not potatoes.

Temperature range: −140°C to 21°C

Not to scale!

How we might live there one day: Mars will almost certainly be the second planet that humans live on. It's (relatively) close to Earth, and it has (mostly frozen) water! But don't pack your bags just yet. Low gravity means colonists' muscles may deteriorate. The thin atmosphere doesn't keep out radiation. There's no oxygen to breathe. And most of Mars is much, much colder than Antarctica. Then again, Mars has a good side, too: Its days are almost the same length as Earth's, so we wouldn't have four months of nighttime at a stretch, like we would on Venus. Its atmosphere may lack oxygen, but it doesn't have anything toxic, either. And on a hot day, Mars' equator is as warm as a nice day on Earth.

Our GIANT foldout didn't even get to Mars.
We have to zoom out again to see it! But first . . .

Jupiter is very, very, very far away from its neighbors. . . .

Now we can see Mars.

It's 206 to 249 million km from the Sun, and it's even farther away from Earth than the first three planets are from each other. But we've sent some robots there!

Here's the asteroid belt. It looks like there's nothing here, but there are a lot of very small somethings here.

Ceres, the biggest thing in the asteroid belt, is a dwarf planet about one fifth as wide as Mercury. Even if we made the asteroids 1,000 times bigger than our scale, you still couldn't see them. If you could see Ceres, though, it would be about here, 382.77 to 445.75 million km from the Sun.

Let's clear up ANOTHER lie.

Remember that first model with the planets way too close together? Well . . .

The planets do NOT orbit the Sun in perfect circles.

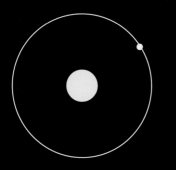

They move in oval shapes called ELLIPSES.

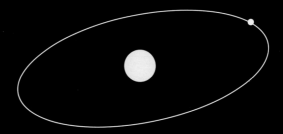

Our scale model had Mercury 57.9 million km away from the Sun, but that's actually its average distance. Mercury can be anywhere from 46 to 69.8 million km away. So instead of **THIS**: •

We should have made Mercury look like **THIS**:

Oh well, too late to go back and change it now.

And speaking of lies, as you might have noticed, we put all the planets in a straight line.

But in real life, they're almost never arranged like that. Usually, they're on different sides of the Sun, which means they're **EVEN FARTHER AWAY** from each other.

This is a pretty good time to fly to Mars.

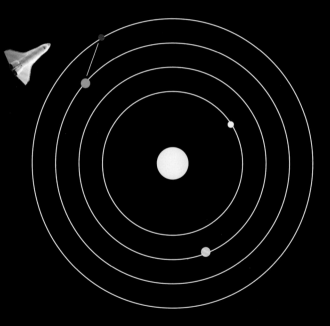

This is not a good time.

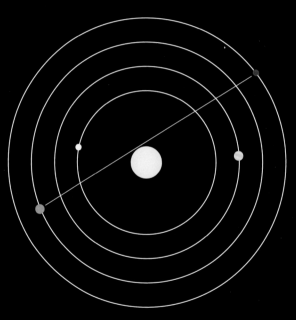

So we've established that this model is wrong and not at all to scale and full of lies.
But at least you get the idea that sometimes the planets are on different sides of the Sun.

Okay, we ALREADY unfolded one model and we only got to Earth. Let's scale down to 1,000,000,000,000 to 1.

SUN   MERCURY   VENUS   EARTH

This is the Sun at one trillionth its true size.

The planets are now 100 times the size they should be,
and you still can't see Mercury very well.

The previous foldout
only got us to here.
We squeezed Earth in by
showing its **CLOSEST**
distance!

Unfold the left and right sides.

So finally we get to Saturn.

Saturn's really, really far away from the Sun. Like, crazy far: 1,353 to 1,515 million km.

Want to hear something wild? The next planet is twice as far away. And it's an even longer trip to the planet after that.

All done? Fold these pages back up and we'll zoom in on . . .

... THE GAS GIANTS at 1,000,000,000-to-1 scale

These next four planets also have a lot in common. They're much, much bigger than the inner planets. They're much, much farther away from the Sun—and from each other. They all have rings, although Saturn is the show-off. And we'll never land an astronaut on any of them because they're all giant balls of gas.

All the planets on this spread are **one billionth** of their actual size, including the familiar faces below.

Europa
(not to scale!)

You get this.

Mercury comes closest to aligning with the Sun's equator, at just 3.38° off.

Earth is 7.16° off, the most of the eight major planets.

Dwarf planet Eris is 44.04° off, which means it's even farther away from the others than it looks in a flat model.

Most of the planets orbit on a ROUGHLY flat plane.

That's because they follow the Sun's equator—but they're all a few degrees off. The distance between two planets can change drastically depending on where they are in their orbits and how their orbits are angled. This is why we mostly talk about the planets' distance from the Sun and not from each other.

Uranus. Neptune. Both so insanely far away, we have to scale down to 10,000,000,000,000 to 1.

At the original 100,000,000-to-1 scale, these six pages would be the width of a soccer field.

SUN   MARS   JUPITER   SATURN

The previous foldout
only got us to here.

Can you see this little speck of dust?
That's the Sun at a ten-trillionth of its actual size.

The planets are now one hundred times this new scale, so you can see . . . well, just
Jupiter and Saturn, really. They only look bigger than the Sun because we're cheating.

Unfold the left and right sides.

Go ahead, giggle about "Uranus." We'll wait.

Days to orbit the Sun:
30,688.5 Earth days (84 years)

Length of day: 17 hours, 14 minutes, 24 seconds

Gravity: 88.6% Earth gravity

Gases present: 83% hydrogen, 15% helium, 2.3% methane

Jokes about Uranus' gases: You know what? Uranus has heard all the jokes. It's heard them so many times. It got old a long time ago.

Moons: 27 moons

How we might live there one day: This one's a long shot. Uranus has a few large moons and a bunch of small ones, but none of them has an atmosphere, which means no oxygen, no water, and nothing to trap heat. Not that they get much heat from the Sun anyway, since they're super far away from it. All of this means Uranus' moons are almost as cold as the empty vacuum of space. Brrr.

Neptune is a much deeper blue than Uranus, and no one knows why.

Days to orbit the Sun: 60,182 (164.8 years)

Length of day: 16 hours, 6 minutes, 36 seconds

Gravity: 114% Earth gravity

Probably tastes like: Blue raspberry

Gases present: 80% hydrogen, 19% helium, 1.5% methane

Moons: 14 moons

How we might live there one day: Only one of Neptune's moons is big enough to build a base on, and that's Triton. And Triton has half as much gravity as our moon, and 1/70,000th as much atmosphere as Earth. Between that and being **VERY FAR AWAY,** it's only 38°C warmer than absolute zero, the coldest possible temperature. We'll stick to the worse-than-Antarctica cold of Mars, thank you very much.

That line under Neptune doesn't belong to Neptune.
It belongs to Pluto.

Pluto hangs out between 4.44 and 7.38 billion km from the Sun. Its orbit is so noncircular, it's sometimes closer than Neptune! (By the way, we're now showing these dwarf planets at a **THOUSAND** times scale . . . and they're still itty bitty.)

Dwarf planets aren't the only thing in this part of the solar system.

There's a whole cloud of smaller stuff called the Kuiper Belt, in a ring around the Sun.
It's one way that scientists define the edge of the solar system.

See that little dot? Uranus.

The first 1.4 billion kilometers from the Sun has six planets and an asteroid belt.

The next 1.4 billion kilometers has Uranus.

It's 2.74 to 3.01 billion km away.

This is Neptune.

4.46 to 4.54 billion km from the Sun.

Its orbit is pretty close to a circle.

Confession time:
We're still lying to you a little bit.

You know how we told you that the planets aren't really in a straight line because they're on different sides of the Sun? There's another reason they aren't in a straight line, and another lie hidden in this model.

This model is flat. The solar system is not.

Once again, books (even this book) have to cheat when they show you the solar system. Because paper is very, very flat. But in fact, the planets orbit the Sun in all different directions.

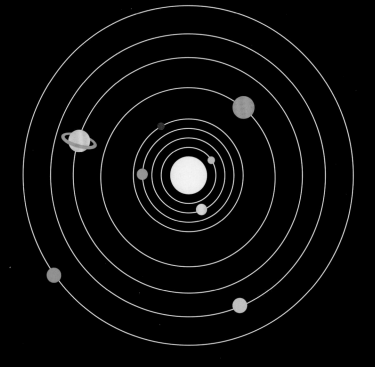

If you look at the solar system from the side, you don't get this:

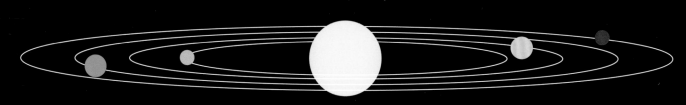

It's easy to spot Jupiter's big red Spot.
It's a never-ending hurricane that's larger than Earth!

Days to orbit the Sun: 4,332.59 Earth days (11.9 years)

Mass: 1.8982 x 10^{27} kg (more than all the other planets put together!)

Length of day: 9 hours, 55 minutes, 30 seconds

Favorite color: Green, actually. We were surprised, too.

Gravity: 252.8% Earth gravity

Gases present: 89% hydrogen, 10% helium, 0.3% methane

Moons: 79 moons. (And counting. Moons are surprisingly good at hiding.)

Temperature range: −161°C to −108°C

How we might live there one day: We won't. Jupiter is made of gas. Its moons, however, are not. The fourth largest, Europa, is about the size of Earth's moon, and its atmosphere is mostly oxygen. Scientists think it might have liquid water trapped under a thick layer of ice. The downside is that Jupiter's radiation would kill an unprotected human in a few months. But the biggest obstacle is also the most exciting: Europa might be home to alien life. Even if they're microscopic, we don't want to interfere with (tiny little) aliens.

We sent probes to Jupiter. Then we figured, why not also go to Saturn? And Uranus and Neptune and Pluto?

In 1973, *Pioneer 10* became the first space probe to reach Jupiter. After *Pioneer 11* reached Jupiter the following year, it kept going and visited Saturn as well. NASA launched *Voyager 1* and *Voyager 2* in 1977; both went to Jupiter and Saturn, and *Voyager 2* kept on going to Uranus and Neptune. In 2006, NASA launched *New Horizons*, which visited Jupiter and then skipped Saturn and the other gas giants before becoming the first probe to visit Pluto in 2015.

All those probes are now very, very, very far away. They will eventually leave the solar system!

Don't feel bad for Jupiter, though.
It has 79 moons to keep it company.

Jupiter's orbit isn't as much of an oval as Mercury's, but it still moves
closer and farther from the Sun: 740.52 to 816.62 million km away.

Jupiter is the biggest planet, but keep in mind:
We cheated and made all the planets 100 times
too big so they'd show up on our map.

Everybody loves Saturn.
It's got those stylish rings.
Jupiter's a little jealous, if we're being honest.

Days to orbit the Sun: 10,759.22 Earth days (29.5 years)

Length of day: 10 hours, 33 minutes, 38 seconds

Gravity: 106.5% Earth gravity

Best friend: Uranus. (Don't tell Jupiter, or its feelings will be hurt.)

Gases present: 96.3% hydrogen, 3.25% helium, 0.45% methane

Moons: 82 moons. (So many, we've only come up with names for 53!)

Temperature range: −185°C to −122°C

How we might live there one day: Saturn is another gas giant we can't live on, with a large moon we might live on. Titan is bigger than Mercury and has a thick atmosphere. In 2005, the *Huygens* probe discovered that it's covered in chunks of ice, which means it has water! The problem? It only gets 1% as much sunlight as Earth, so it's incredibly cold: −179.6°C at most. That's so cold, there are rivers and lakes of liquid methane, which is a gas on Earth. Not something you want to swim in! But methane can be used as rocket fuel, so Titan could be a launchpad for ships to explore even farther away.

Wait, is that really it for the solar system?

So this is weird, because we're at the end of the solar system, but we're also not. That's because scientists have several ways of measuring where that is. One is the Kuiper Belt, but another is the heliosphere. The Sun is constantly shooting out plasma particles called the solar wind. Eventually the solar wind slows down and stops—much farther away than the dwarf planets—to form a sort of bubble around the Sun: the heliosphere.

And then there's the Oort cloud. We'll get to the Oort cloud.

Remember *Voyager 1*, which flew to Jupiter and Saturn and is now on its way out of the solar system? If we wanted to show its current distance, we'd have to fold out four more pages before we get to it.

Fold these pages back up
and let's check out . . .

. . . THE DWARF PLANETS at

20,000,000-to-1 scale

This scale is five times bigger than the one we used to look closely at the inner planets. No probes have visited the last three dwarf planets yet, so the best photos we have are these blurry splotches taken through a telescope.

You remember Ceres.

The other dwarfs are very, very, very, far away, but Ceres lives in the asteroid belt and is only very, very far away.

Days to orbit the Sun: 1,682 Earth days

Length of day: 9 hours, 4 minutes

Gravity: 2.9% Earth gravity

Moons: None

How we might live there one day: It'd be pretty tough. If you weighed 100 pounds on Earth, you'd weigh under 3 pounds on Ceres, slightly more than a large guinea pig. Every time you took a step, you'd go flying through the air. And your muscles would get so little exercise, you'd waste away pretty quickly. We'll probably never live on a planet this small. (But we might send spaceships to the asteroid belt and then mine the asteroids for metal to build more spaceships with.)

The Moon is bigger than all these mini planets.

We decided what to call Pluto. We're still not sure about Charon.

Days to orbit the Sun: Same as Pluto

Length of day: Same as Pluto

Gravity: 2.9% Earth gravity

We're three dwarf planets in, and we're already lying to you again. Charon isn't a planet—it's Pluto's biggest moon. Except maybe it is a dwarf planet. Or maybe not. Scientists can't decide. Some think Pluto is a small planet with a moon that's half as big (across) as Pluto itself. But some think they're two dwarf planets that hang out together (along with Pluto's other four moons).

The same side of Charon always faces Pluto (just like the same side of our moon always faces Earth). But unlike our moon, Charon revolves around Pluto at the same rate that Pluto rotates around its own axis. So one side of Pluto can always see Charon and the other side never can.

Haumea wins the solar system's least-flattering photo contest.

Days to orbit the Sun: 103,410 Earth days (283 years)

Length of day: 4 hours

Gravity: 2.4% Earth gravity

Moons: Hi'iaka and Namaka

Egg-shaped Haumea spins so quickly that it bulges way out at the equator. It's also so far away that this blur-tastic photo is the best we've got. But the white outline is its actual size at our 20,000,000-to-1 scale.

Haumea and Makemake have oval-shaped orbits, too.

These two and Pluto are constantly taking turns at being closest to the Sun.
Haumea is 5.18 to 7.72 billion km away, and Makemake is 5.7 to 7.89 billion km.

So that's it for the solar system.

Sure, there's other, mostly smaller stuff: asteroids, comets, those UFOs the government is keeping secret. Still, if we're talking about planets, we're done.

When Pluto got thrown out of the planet club, it started its own club.

Days to orbit the Sun: 90,560 Earth days (248 years)

Length of day: 6 Earth days, 9 hours, 17 minutes

Gravity: 6.3% Earth gravity

Moons: 5 moons (counting Charon)

From 1930, when Pluto was discovered, until 2005, when Eris was discovered, our model of the solar system had nine planets. But Pluto—the smallest, farthest planet, with its very oval-shaped orbit—never quite fit in. So in 2006, scientists demoted Pluto to a dwarf planet. A lot of people were angry that we went from nine planets to eight. But in fact, we went from nine planets to at least thirteen—so many we needed a new category.

How we might live there one day: We're going to stop doing this one because these other dwarf planets are so small, so cold, and so far away that none of them make particularly good places to live. Sorry, dwarf planets.

Makemake doesn't rhyme with "cake."

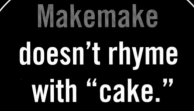

It's pronounced mah-kay-mah-kay. But who knows? There could be cake there!

Days to orbit the Sun: 111,845 Earth days (306 years)

Length of day: 22 hours, 29 minutes

Gravity: 5.7% Earth gravity

Moons: 1 . . . maybe? Scientists spotted something 20,000 km away from Makemake, but they're not yet sure if it was a moon or a passing asteroid.

Still mad about Pluto? Blame Eris.

Days to orbit the Sun:
204,199 Earth days (559 years)

Length of day: 25 hours, 54 minutes

Gravity: 8.4% Earth gravity

Moons: Dysnomia

We're lucky someone noticed Eris. It goes much, much, much farther away than Pluto. But they're about the same size, so astronomers decided that either both should be planets or neither should be. Haumea and Makemake had also been found by then, so scientists made a new category: the dwarf planets!

BARNARD'S STAR LUHMAN 16 A and B WISE 0855-0714

One thing about the stars.

Remember how we talked about the planets rarely being in a straight line? All these stars are **NEVER** in a straight line. They're not close to each other at all. You'd have to go in a different direction to get to each of them. We only put them in a line to compare their distances from us (and fit them in the book)!

The nearest star is actually three stars.

Alpha Centauri A and B and Proxima Centauri all orbit each other. They are so far away, their light takes 4 years and 133 days to reach Earth. A and B are each about the size of our sun. Proxima is only twice the size of Jupiter, but it's the most exciting since it has a planet similar to Earth. If humans ever live among the stars, Proxima Centauri will probably be our first stop.

PROXIMA CENTAURI

ALPHA CENTAURI
A and B

So that's it for the planets. Except maybe not?

You already saw these two pages in the last foldout—but now we've added some new stuff. Scientists are still deciding whether or not these extra things are official dwarf planets. If you're reading this in the future, maybe some of them will be. (The orbits are at the same scale as the last foldout, but the planets themselves are enlarged. We wanted to make sure you could see them!)

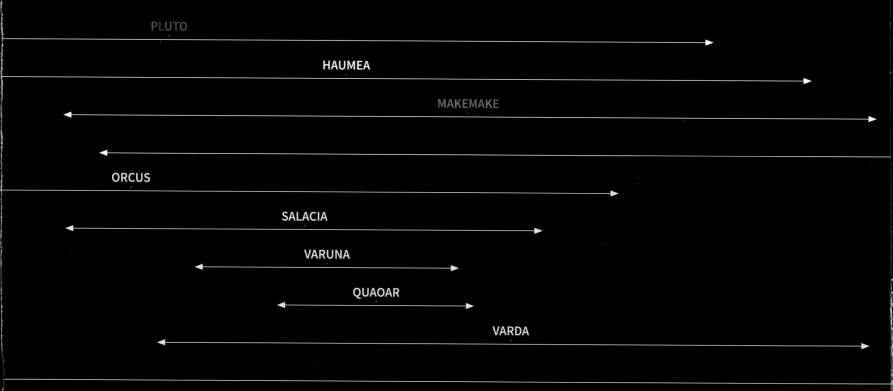

And how do you tell a small planet from a large rock, anyway?

A planet has to do three things: 1) orbit the Sun, 2) be spherical, and 3) "clear the neighborhood," which means there aren't any similarly sized objects around its orbit. Objects that do 1 and 2 but not 3, like all these Kuiper Belt buddies, get to be dwarf planets. (Don't have enough gravity for a rounded shape, either? Then you're probably just an asteroid.) Mike Brown, codiscoverer of Eris, thinks there are around 230 "nearly certain"-to-"probable" dwarfs out there besides the official five. These two pages show the biggest ones that already have names. If you add $2002MS_4$, $2002AW_{197}$, $2003AZ_{84}$, $2013FY_{27}$, $2002UX_{25}$, $2004GV_9$, $2005RN_{43}$, and $2014UZ_{224}$, you'll have his top 15.

ERIS

This way to Sedna. Pack some snacks!

Remember how incredibly far from the Sun Eris goes? Ninety-four times farther than Earth, to be exact? Sedna is almost that far at its closest. At its farthest? Sedna goes 9.5 times farther than Eris. It goes 7.74 times farther than the heliosphere! Which means, if you consider the heliosphere the edge of the solar system, we might have a dwarf planet that only comes to visit once in a while.

GONGGONG

So far, every foldout has been ten times
the previous scale. Not this time. This time
we're going to 100,000,000,000,000,000 to 1.

Unfold this side to see some stars.

This dot is the entire solar system at a hundred quadrillion to one.

That's **TEN THOUSAND** times the last scale. At the scale of our first foldout, this page would be long enough to build a bridge over Lake Erie, or from Ireland to England. Three pages would reach from New York to Boston.

. . . that is, unless you count the Oort cloud.

Scientists aren't completely certain this region of icy objects exists, but if it does, it starts beyond the heliosphere—and ends anywhere from 10,000 to 100,000 astronomical units (AU) away from the Sun. The distance from Earth to the Sun is just 1 single AU!

And that's it: There are only 15 stars within 10 light-years of Earth.

LUYTEN 726-8 A and B

LALANDE 21185

SIRIUS A and B

359

ROSS 154

ROSS 248

But just in case you'd prefer a **HUNDRED BILLION** stars or so . . .

That's 2,000,000,000,000,000,000,000 to 1.

It's pretty big.

The spiral disk is about 100,000 light-years across, not counting its massive halo of more stars, plus what scientists suspect is lots of dark matter. Our sun takes **230 MILLION YEARS** to revolve around the center. The last time we were at this location, dinosaurs were a new type of animal.

And it's filled with planets.

We discovered the first exoplanet in 1995. Since then, we've found **THOUSANDS**. They're tricky to find, since planets don't shine like stars. But sometimes one will reflect starlight or cross in front of a star and show us its silhouette. Some planets have so much gravity, we can see their stars wobble as they go by. And massive gas giants can give off enough radiation for us to detect.

You are here

26,500 light-years from the center, give or take.

"Goldilocks worlds" are the most exciting.

They're not so hot that everything melts and not so cold that everything freezes. Maybe—just maybe—these "just right" planets support alien life. Maybe we could live there one day! Sure, we'd also need the right amount of gravity and atmosphere, and ideally some water to drink and oxygen to breathe. But temperature's a good first thing to check, and it's something we CAN check from here.

The Milky Way has **billions** more exoplanets just waiting to be discovered.

They are all very, very, very far away.

The Experiment, LLC
220 East 23rd Street, Suite 600
New York, NY 10010-4658
theexperimentpublishing.com

THE EXPERIMENT and its colophon are registered trademarks of The Experiment, LLC. Many of the designations used by manufacturers and sellers to distinguish their products are claimed as trademarks. Where those designations appear in this book and The Experiment was aware of a trademark claim, the designations have been capitalized.

The Experiment's books are available at special discounts when purchased in bulk for premiums and sales promotions as well as for fundraising or educational use. For details, contact us at info@theexperimentpublishing.com.

Library of Congress Cataloging-in-Publication Data available on request

ISBN 978-1-61519-777-4
Ebook ISBN 978-1-61519-778-1

Cover and text design by Beth Bugler
Cover photograph by Adobe Stock

Manufactured in China

First printing August 2022
10 9 8 7 6 5 4 3 2 1

IMAGE CREDITS

Sun: SOHO-EIT Consortium/ESA/NASA.

Mercury: NASA/JHUAPL/Carnegie Institution of Washington.

Venus, Uranus, Neptune, Makemake, Milky Way: NASA/JPL-Caltech.

Earth, Voyager 1: NASA.

Moon: NASA/GSFC/Arizona State University.

Mars: NASA/JPL/USGS.

Deimos, Phobos: University of Arizona/HiRISE-LPL.

Ceres: NASA/JPL-Caltech/UCLA/MPS/DLR/IDA.

Jupiter: NASA/ESA/STScI/A. Simon (GSFC)/M. H. Wong (University of California, Berkeley)/the OPAL team.

Europa: NASA/JPL/DLR.

Saturn: NASA/ESA/A. Simon (GSFC)/M. H. Wong (University of California, Berkeley)/the OPAL Team.

Pluto, Charon: NASA/JHUAPL/SwRI.

Haumea: W.M. Keck Observatory/Caltech/Mike Brown et al.

Eris: NASA/ESA/Mike Brown (Caltech).

All other photographs: Adobe Stock.